GROUP
⟶ *Video Experience* ⟵

TONY EVANS
RAISING
KINGDOM
KIDS

GIVING YOUR CHILD
A LIVING FAITH

D0720978

TYNDALE HOUSE PUBLISHERS, INC.
CAROL STREAM, ILLINOIS

Raising Kingdom Kids Group Video Experience
Participant's Guide

Copyright © 2015 Focus on the Family
ISBN: 978-1-62405-408-2

Based on the book *Raising Kingdom Kids* by Dr. Tony Evans, © 2014 Tony Evans. Published by Tyndale House Publishers, Inc., and Focus on the Family.

Focus on the Family and the accompanying logo and design are federally registered trademarks of Focus on the Family, 8605 Explorer Drive, Colorado Springs, CO 80920.

A Focus on the Family book published by Tyndale House Publishers, Carol Stream, Illinois 60188

TYNDALE is a registered trademark of Tyndale House Publishers, Inc. Tyndale's quill logo is a trademark of Tyndale House Publishers, Inc.

Cover design by Jennifer Ghionzoli
Cover skyline photo copyright © PhotoDisc. All rights reserved.
Cover photograph taken by Stephen Vosloo. © Focus on the Family.

Printed in the United States of America
3 4 5 6 7 / 21

CONTENTS

WELCOME, KINGDOM PARENTS!

"It's far easier to shape a child than to repair an adult," according to Dr. Tony Evans. Creating a kingdom mind-set in your home may sound like more than you can handle. But by starting with simple principles and starting today, you can produce benefits that will last a lifetime!

Raising kids who recognize and retain their identity as children of the King launches healthy adults who have the capacity to stand strong in their faith. By going through the DVD sessions and this guide, you'll be able to trade reactive parenting for intentional parenting and marvel at the difference. You'll also grow in confidence as you discover your worth as a parent, based on God's Word.

At the core of each session is a video presentation featuring Dr. Tony Evans, author of *Raising Kingdom Kids*. Dr. Evans's inspired teaching will give parents new insights into biblical principles as well as assurance that God will equip every kingdom parent to be a transformational kingdom parent.

To make these truths come alive, you'll find these sections in each session:

The Gathering

Read this brief excerpt to focus on the subject at hand. Answer the questions that follow the passage. If you run out of time, finish the section at home.

Show Time!

Use this section as you view and think about the DVD presentation; it includes thought-provoking questions and biblical input.

Transformation Moments

This brief wrap-up will help you find encouragement and usually presents a challenge to try this week.

Note: The DVD presentations and this guide are intended as general advice only, and not meant to replace clinical counseling, medical treatment, legal counsel, or pastoral guidance.

Focus on the Family maintains a referral network of Christian counselors. For information, call 1-800-A FAMILY (1-800-232-6459) and ask for the counseling department.

1

◇ ◇ ◇

THIS ISN'T THE MAGIC KINGDOM

The Main Point

Kingdom parenting is God's call for all parents; it is a calling set forth in Genesis.

The Gathering

To find out more about the true purpose of kingdom parenting from a biblical perspective, read the following excerpt from *Raising Kingdom Kids*. If you have time, answer the questions that appear at the end of the selection. Or you can finish the section at home.

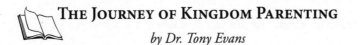

THE JOURNEY OF KINGDOM PARENTING
by Dr. Tony Evans

Parents, some of you are just beginning your journey in raising kingdom kids, and your eyes are filled with the bliss of those people standing in line to board an enjoyable ride at Disneyland. Others of you have teenagers who are walking with the Lord and on the right path, but you are seeking wisdom on how to guide them through the transition from the youthful innocence of Fantasyland to the more turbulent times waiting in Tomorrowland. Still others may have children who have walked away from the Lord. Their fairy tales have morphed into tragedies, and you want to know how to point your kids back home. And others are facing the challenges of a blended family whose members may not even want to be at the park at all.

This *Raising Kingdom Kids Group Video Experience* will meet each of you in a different place on your parenting path. Regardless of where you are, if you apply the principles we are about to explore, you will experience their fruits in your home. By intentionally applying these principles, you will reinforce one of the primary traits of a healthy home: honor. You will honor your kids by placing a high enough value on them to warrant the time and energy needed to parent well.[1]

What stage of parenting are you in? What is one positive change you'd like to see in the lives of your children as a result of experiencing the *Raising Kingdom Kids* curriculum? What does it mean to honor children by "placing a high enough value on them to warrant the time and energy needed to parent well"?

Show Time!

In session 1 of the *Raising Kingdom Kids Group Video Experience*, Dr. Tony Evans uses "the Magic Kingdom" as a metaphor for explaining the difference between purposeful kingdom parenting and distracted worldly parenting.

◇ ◇ ◇

After viewing Tony Evans's presentation, "This Isn't the Magic Kingdom," use the following questions to help you think through what you saw and heard.

1. Dr. Evans uses an extended metaphor to compare Disney's Magic Kingdom with God's kingdom. In the Magic Kingdom, there are many distractions such as shows, games, rides, food stands, and gift shops.

   What are some of the things in your life that distract you from fully participating as a parent in God's kingdom? Check the box of the ones that apply to you or write in your own.

   ❐ work demands
   ❐ television or movies
   ❐ computer activities
   ❐ shopping
   ❐ sports and recreation
   ❐ maintaining the household

❏ care for elderly parents
❏ hanging out with friends
❏ church activities
❏ education or vocational training
❏ reading material (books, online articles, blogs, magazines)
❏ volunteer work
❏ cooking
❏ other _____
❏ other _____
❏ other _____

2. Dr. Evans claims, "We're paying a high price tag in our culture today for the breakdown of the family and the loss of the innocence of the next generation." He tells the story of meeting two single mothers who have taken tragic measures (prostitution and selling drugs) to earn money to care for their families.

   In what areas has your family or extended family "paid the price tag" for the breakdown of the family? for the loss of innocence of the next generation?

Which of those broken areas in your family would you most like to see redeemed through God's kingdom principles for families?

3. In the following space, write what would have been your personal definition of kingdom parenting if you hadn't heard DVD session 1.

In the DVD, Dr. Evans explains that parenting is not merely a social enterprise. It is a spiritual and theological imperative. It is the responsibility of parents to raise children in such a way that the stamp of God is on them, so that the next generation reveals God's likeness in human history. Dr. Evans's formal definition of kingdom parenting is this: **Kingdom parenting is intentionally overseeing the generational transfer of the faith in such a way that children learn to consistently live under the rule of God.**

Rewrite your definition to include any of Dr. Evans's points that you may have omitted and now believe are essential to kingdom parenting.

4. In the story about the wild pigs being corralled, the corral builders lured the pigs in with food. What are the "lures" the world uses to entice your children away from God's kingdom? Check the box of any that apply to you or write in your own.

- ❏ alcohol or other substance abuse
- ❏ easy money through illegal activity
- ❏ acclaim for achievement in sports, academics, or music
- ❏ recreation
- ❏ fashion
- ❏ jobs
- ❏ volunteer work
- ❏ computer diversions such as games
- ❏ social media
- ❏ food
- ❏ pornography or sex

❑ laziness

❑ gossip

❑ toys

❑ boyfriend or girlfriend

❑ reading material (books, online articles, blogs, magazines)

❑ other _____

❑ other _____

❑ other _____

Dr. Evans claims, "The culture wants your children. The culture wants my children. The culture wants to control us. The culture wants to dominate us. You have to fight for your family."

List at least two ways you can help your children avoid being corralled by worldly values this week.

5. Nehemiah 4:14 says, "After I looked . . . [at the fallen wall and the people defending it], I stood up and said to the nobles, the officials and the rest of the people, 'Don't be afraid of . . . [our

enemies who want to kill us]. Remember the LORD, who is great and awesome, and fight for your brothers, your sons and your daughters, your wives and your homes.'" Nehemiah was under both a physical and a spiritual attack. The Jewish families were in danger. Nehemiah called the families together and asked them to fight for the future.

Nehemiah and the Jews had to prepare and plan for battle in two ways: spiritually and practically. Nehemiah asked for God's protection, and he also prepared the families for battle.

In what ways are you currently fighting the spiritual battle for your children?

In what practical ways are you defending your family from the culture?

In what ways would you like to better prepare your family for the culture war?

6. Read the following excerpt from *Raising Kingdom Kids*, and reflect on the questions at the end.

THE BUBBLE
by Priscilla Shirer

[My parents, Tony and Lois Evans,] constructed a bubble of sorts for us to live in. Home life was padded with instruction in God's Word, discipline in life lessons (such as saving and tithing our money), manners ("No elbows on the table!"), and good work ethics. We had lots of fun with our friends, but we played mostly at our home instead of theirs because my parents were so careful about the kinds of influences we might encounter somewhere else. Sure, that meant taking on the exhausting work of having a dozen sweaty kids track muddy prints in and out of the kitchen for snacks and Kool-Aid during games of basketball and Ping-Pong. But our parents did it for a reason. And they did it for us.

When we weren't at home, we were at church or at school—a simple, quaint, Christian school that reinforced the lessons taught at home. Public school came during our high school years. But even then, my parents were very involved in our studies and our friendships. They were watching, stewarding, shepherding.

They just seemed to have this knowing inside—a deep, inner consciousness about the culture. They knew their job as parents couldn't be passive. They knew they needed to fight aggressively against the low values and standards of the common crowd, the crude lasciviousness that was trying to seep into our minds and hearts, our attitudes and opinions, our actions and emotions.

So they put on their gloves . . . and fought.

And now that I'm older, I'm grateful for it. I can see it all more clearly. I recognize the wrinkles around the eyes that were whittled out of long nights and loving discipline.

In fact, I never thought I'd say this, but . . . I want those wrinkles, too. And I'm working on them as hard as I can.

That's why I'm sitting these three sons of mine around a dinner table tonight, just as my parents did, and teaching them God's Word. I won't allow myself to be lulled to sleep and disengage from their education, their friendships, their influences. And together with their father, I'll be intentional and purposeful in their lives every precious day that God gives us to share with them under our roof, until they spread their wings and fly out of this nest—off on their own where, hopefully, the cycle will continue.[2]

Based on this excerpt, what would you say are three key qualities of a kingdom parent? Which qualities come naturally to you? Which do you need to develop in order to become a stronger kingdom parent?

Transformation Moments
Read the following passage from the book of Ephesians. Answer the questions that follow the passage. If you run out of time, finish this section at home.

 ## THE ARMOR OF GOD

Finally, be strong in the Lord and in the strength of His might. Put on the full armor of God, so that you will be able to stand firm against the schemes of the devil. For our struggle is not against flesh and blood, but against the rulers, against the powers, against the world forces of this darkness, against the spiritual forces of wickedness in the heavenly places. Therefore, take up the full armor of God, so that you will be able to resist in the evil day, and having done everything, to stand firm. Stand firm therefore, having girded your loins with truth, and having put on the breastplate of righteousness, and having shod your feet with the preparation of the gospel of peace; in addition to all, taking up the shield of faith with which you will be able to extinguish all the flaming arrows of the evil one. And take the helmet of salvation, and the sword of the Spirit, which is the word of God.

With all prayer and petition pray at all times in the Spirit, and with this in view, be on the alert with all perseverance and petition for all the saints. (Ephesians 6:10–18)

This passage from Ephesians describes what a kingdom parent should focus on. What are some ways parents can guard their children against a spiritual attack from the culture? How would you rewrite this passage in your own words? How does the last sentence of the passage apply to raising kingdom kids?

2

◇ ◇ ◇

"BUT DANIEL . . ."

The Main Point
Daniel's life shows how someone with a kingdom mind-set should respond to the culture.

The Gathering
To find out more about the importance of raising children who can successfully handle culture clashes, read the following excerpt from *Raising Kingdom Kids*. If you have time, answer the questions that appear at the end of the selection. Or you can finish the section at home.

 ## SENDING A SON TO "SIN CITY"
by Dr. Tony Evans

I'll admit it—I was fearful when Anthony moved to Hollywood. My concern was rooted in the idea that such a broad level of exposure to the secular world would invade his Christian worldview and erode his values. I had similar concerns when our daughter Priscilla started participating in (and winning) beauty pageants at college, and when our son Jonathan was signed by the NFL and thrust into an environment that included being surrounded by people who partied and drank a lot.

At these junctures, I always wondered, *Did we raise them with enough of a kingdom mind-set to resist the world's temptations?* And while I'm sure none of our kids were squeaky clean and never made a wrong choice, by and large they made it through those times strong.

Parents, one of the hardest parts of parenting is letting your child go out into a world that you no longer can control or heavily influence. But each child will eventually have to make his or her own decisions. That's why it is so critical that you provide your children with a deep foundation while they are still with you, making sure you have equipped them with what they need in order to live as a Daniel in their own Babylon.[1]

In your parenting journey, tell about a time when you had to let your child enter a situation in which he or she could morally or spiritually fail. What fears or concerns did you have? What was the result of the challenge your child faced? What does it mean to "equip your children with what they need in order to live as a Daniel in their own Babylon"?

Show Time!

In session 2 of the *Raising Kingdom Kids Group Video Experience*, Dr. Tony Evans talks about developing a kingdom mind-set inside the minds of children and why it is important for kingdom kids to be able to withstand cultural values that conflict with biblical values.

◊ ◊ ◊

After viewing Tony Evans's presentation, "But Daniel . . . ," use the following questions to help you think through what you saw and heard.

1. How does our society select promising young men and women? Who are the "Daniels" in our high schools and how are they lauded? Is it your goal to have your children identified as one of the best and brightest?

   According to Dr. Evans, what are some of the spiritual dangers that gifted, talented, or successful kids face in our culture today?

2. Dr. Evans claims, "Our culture wants to . . . remove the God-consciousness that you may try to instill in [your kids] and make them secular in their thinking, secular in their orientation."

   In what areas do you see the culture trying to secularize your kids? Do you think Dr. Evans is exaggerating the spiritual danger that the culture's influence has on Christian kids? Explain your answer.

3. Dr. Evans encourages parents to give their children "God-names" or a "God-stamp." Parents can do this in literal and figurative ways. Consider the following list. Put a check in the box if you have marked or would like to mark your kids with the following "stamps."

   ❐ My kids have biblical names or nicknames that reflect our family's adherence to Scripture.

   ❐ My kids understand that our family has spiritual standards that are higher than the standards of the culture.

   ❐ My kids understand that by adhering to biblical standards, things will most likely go well for them and they will avoid many of life's pitfalls.

❐ My kids understand that by adhering to biblical standards they will most certainly face opposition and unpopularity.

❐ My kids know the stories of biblical heroes and draw strength of character from the biblical accounts.

❐ My kids know that their family and church communities will support them when they remain faithful to God's culture.

❐ My kids see me and/or my spouse making choices that adhere to kingdom values.

❐ My kids have peers, like Daniel's friends, who also hold to biblical values and standards.

❐ Bible study is a high priority in our home.

4. At Trailways Bus Station, Dr. Evans faced a trial. What were the short-term consequences of his choice to work the entire shift without sleeping? What were the long-term rewards?

Do you really believe that God finds favor with those who obey Him? How has that principle played out in your life?

Read Psalm 5:12 and 84:11 and rewrite them in your own words.

5. Dr. Evans challenges listeners by saying, "Your job and my job as parents is to put [an oxygen] tank on our kids' backs, so that they can breathe in a secular culture." In practical terms, list ways you can help your children "breathe in a secular culture" this week.

6. Read the following excerpt from *Raising Kingdom Kids*, and reflect on the questions at the end.

LESSONS LEARNED IN LA

by Anthony Evans Jr.

My phone rang, and on the other end was someone from NBC asking if I would come to Hollywood and be a part of a new show called *The Voice*. That's how it all started for me. Until that time, a couple of years ago, I had never been immersed in secular culture. I never knew the meaning of "living outside of the palace walls." When I received an invitation to be on *The Voice* and then decided to move to Los Angeles, I was confused. I had never performed outside of our church, and I wondered if it was wrong to live and work in such a secular environment. I will never forget calling my dad as I tried to figure this all out and hearing him say to me in the first three minutes of our conversation, "As long as you don't compromise your faith, I want you to go and have a great time." Those were the words that freed me up to experience what I consider to have been a life-altering experience.

I now know what it means to literally have to make a choice to be countercultural daily, because most of my friends in LA aren't Christians.

They're confused by what "we" do in church and turned off by how judgmental they consider "us" to be.

It would be very easy to adapt to a new way of thinking in a town like this. But, there are a few things my parents did that bring me back to my core belief system whenever it's challenged. If you're wondering what they did, I can tell you for sure that it had nothing to do with pastoring a ten-thousand-member church, being on more than five hundred radio stations, or having countless books published and numerous invitations to speak. All of these things are inconsequential to me as the son of "well-known Christian parents." What my parents did is nothing other than live an example that I now have engraved into my consciousness. It was watching my parents make decisions to follow the Lord in spite of circumstances. It was the time we spent around the table as they taught me the meaning of making daily decisions to acknowledge the presence of God in my life. At times, just like any "training," it definitely felt rhetorical, but now "living outside the palace" has given me an opportunity to actually experience this training as a reflex. I find myself recalling Scripture and making decisions as a reflex due to the training that I received—just like any athlete repeats a motion until it becomes muscle memory, until it's recalled without having to "think" about it. This is what my parents did. They actually lived and trained us up in the way we should go (see Proverbs 22:6). And this training, although hard at

times, has given me an unwavering example of what i'
looks like to trust in the Lord with my whole heart.[2]

Based on this excerpt, what were two things that Tony and Lois Evans did that influenced Anthony Jr. to stand firm in his faith after he moved to LA?

Transformation Moments

Read the following story from the book of Daniel. Answer the questions that follow the passage. If you run out of time, finish this section at home. Begin by reading the summary of Daniel 6:1–9:

> King Darius's advisors set a trap for Daniel because they were jealous of his influence. The advisors (satraps) tricked the king into creating a law that, in effect, would make it illegal for Daniel to pray to God.

DANIEL AND THE LIONS' DEN

Now when Daniel knew that the document was signed, he entered his house (now in his roof chamber he had windows open toward Jerusalem); and he continued kneeling on his knees three times a day, praying and giving thanks before his God, as he had been doing previously. Then these men came by agreement and found Daniel making petition and supplication before his God. Then they approached and spoke before the king about the king's injunction, "Did you not sign an injunction that any man who makes a petition to any god or man besides you, O king, for thirty days, is to be cast into the lions' den?" The king replied, "The statement is true, according to the law of the Medes and Persians, which may not be revoked." Then they answered and spoke before the king, "Daniel, who is one of the exiles from Judah, pays no attention to you, O king, or to the injunction which you signed, but keeps making his petition three times a day."

Then, as soon as the king heard this statement, he was deeply distressed and set his mind on delivering Daniel; and even until sunset he kept exerting himself to rescue him. Then these men came by agreement to the king and said to the king, "Recognize, O king, that it is a law of the Medes and Persians that no injunction or statute which the king establishes may be changed."

Then the king gave orders, and Daniel was brought in and cast into the lions' den. The king spoke and said to Daniel, "Your God whom you constantly serve will Himself deliver you." A stone was brought and laid over the mouth of the den; and the king sealed it with his own signet ring and with the signet rings of his nobles, so that nothing would be changed in regard to Daniel. Then the king went off to his palace and spent the night fasting, and no entertainment was brought before him; and his sleep fled from him.

Then the king arose at dawn, at the break of day, and went in haste to the lions' den. When he had come near the den to Daniel, he cried out with a troubled voice. The king spoke and said to Daniel, "Daniel, servant of the living God, has your God, whom you constantly serve, been able to deliver you from the lions?" Then Daniel spoke to the king, "O king, live forever! My God sent His angel and shut the lions' mouths and they have not harmed me, inasmuch as I was found innocent before Him; and also toward you, O king, I have committed no crime." Then the king was very pleased and gave orders for Daniel to be taken up out of the den. So Daniel was taken up out of the den and no injury whatever was found on him, because he had trusted in his God. The king then gave orders, and they brought those men who had maliciously accused Daniel, and they cast them, their children and their wives into the lions' den; and they had not reached the bottom of the den before the lions overpowered them and crushed all their bones.

Then Darius the king wrote to all the peoples, nations and men of every language who were living in all the land: "May your peace abound! I make a decree that in all the dominion of my kingdom men are to fear and tremble before the God of Daniel. (Daniel 6:10–26)

This story of Daniel reveals the same principles Dr. Evans pointed out about Daniel. What was the God-stamp that Daniel refused to give up? What were the short-term consequences of his being counterculture? What were the long-term benefits? How far did Daniel's influence reach because he found favor with God?

3

◇ ◇ ◇

TRANSFER THE
KINGDOM BATON

The Main Point

Kingdom parents must transfer the baton of faith to the next generations.

The Gathering

To find out more about how to pass the faith baton effectively, read the following excerpt from *Raising Kingdom Kids*. If you have time, answer the questions that appear at the end of the selection. Or you can finish the section at home.

TRAINING HARD
by Dr. Tony Evans

It takes faith to raise a kingdom family. It takes complete and total dedication to God's Word and His ways. It takes intimacy with Christ and fellowship with the Holy Spirit. It takes the intentional training and discipleship of your children and keeping them ever before God in a heart of prayer. No parent will ever do this perfectly. I know I didn't—I made many mistakes. But that's the great thing about God. When you commit your ways to Him and make His will and glory the desire of your heart, He makes up the difference in all the places you lack. If your kids have gone off course and you have done all that God has asked you to do, then pray for a strong wind from heaven to blow them back to Him. Make sure you keep the light on so they will always know that home eagerly awaits their return (Luke 15:11–32).[1]

For you, what is the most difficult thing about raising children? In what ways is parenting like training for a marathon? In what ways is parenting like training for a 4 x 100 meter relay race?

Show Time!

In session 3 of the *Raising Kingdom Kids Group Video Experience*, Dr. Tony Evans encourages parents to pass the baton of faith. He explains about teaching your children how to have a biblical worldview.

◇ ◇ ◇

After viewing Tony Evans's presentation, "Transfer the Kingdom Baton," use the following questions to help you think through what you saw and heard.

1. Dr. Evans uses the metaphor of sunglasses to explain what a kingdom mind-set or worldview is like. A popular saying is "seeing the world through rose-colored glasses." What type of lenses do you wear when you're filtering information? What type of glasses do your children wear? Who, besides you, has given your children worldview glasses to wear? To stretch the metaphor further, do your children see the world through bifocals—part biblical and part worldly? What can you do to correct their vision so that they clearly see God in every area of life?

2. A second metaphor Dr. Evans uses is that of an umbrella. He compares God's blessing through covenant to an umbrella, which doesn't stop the rain but deflects it so that we don't get wet. What areas of life "rain" on you and your children? How would you describe the spiritual umbrella in your family life? Check the response that best fits your family:

   ❒ Our umbrella is broken. It won't open; it's ribs are crooked and there are holes in the fabric.

   ❒ Our umbrella is in the closet. It works, but we often forget to bring it with us. Every so often we get caught in the rain.

   ❒ We carry umbrellas everywhere. I have one in the car trunk, in the front closet, and one at work. Sometimes a few sprinkles get on us, but for the most part, we're covered.

3. When God blesses families by transferring the blessing promise through generations, the transmission is not without problems for the receivers. Dr. Evans points out that even though the Israelites were getting ready to enter into God's promise, there were problems in the Promised Land.

   What or who are the "Canaanites" in your family scenario? In what areas are you going to have to trust that God will take care of the problems by acting in faith? Or, if you've already seen God at work in your family, write that below.

4. Dr. Evans uses four more metaphors to explain kingdom parenting. Choose one to elaborate on in your own words or develop your own kingdom parenting metaphor. (Here are two ideas: Raising kingdom kids should be like serving in a handball court. Fearing God is like preparing to sail on the ocean.)

- Parenting should be like putting your kids in a pinball machine. Whatever they bump into bounces them toward God.
- Fearing God is like fearing electricity. You should respect its power and know not to mess with the outlets.
- Parents should hook their children to a metaphorical bungee cord. No matter how far or how fast the children go, the bungee cord will always bring the kids back to their launching place.

- Parents are like water or air filters, catching
  contaminates before their children are exposed to
  them.

5. Focus on the Family has a concept called Gen3. That's parents
   reaching out to three generations: their generation, their children, and their grandchildren. What are some of the things
   you'll do differently with your grandkids than you did with
   your kids? Or, if your kids are still young, what are your parents doing now that you want to emulate? What is your plan
   for reaching your grandchildren with the kingdom message?

6. Read the following excerpt from *Raising Kingdom Kids*, and reflect on the questions at the end.

PASSING ON SALVATION
by Dr. Tony Evans

The starting point for transferring faith, of course, is the salvation of your children. The greatest thing parents can do for their children is to lead them to the Lord. As soon as your child has the cognitive ability to understand both sin and the gospel, you have the opportunity to bring that child to a saving knowledge of Jesus Christ.

Be careful, though, not to rush this process; far too many children have no recollection of their salvation experience because they were so young when it happened. As you seek to communicate the gospel to them, children need to truly understand for themselves both sin and their need for forgiveness. In addition, after they are saved, make sure you do not pressure them to get baptized, but rather allow them the opportunity to fully comprehend what baptism expresses publicly. That way they can initiate this declaration of their faith—as well as remember it when they get older.

The single greatest reason why we are losing our young people today is that the home is no longer the place where faith is transferred. Parents, the primary purpose of the home is the evangelization and discipleship of your children. You cannot outsource this vital component in the rearing of your children. Their discipleship requires time and commitment, even though your time and commitment might be divided among too many things already.

I struggled greatly in this area during the first decade of our family. I had a hard time choosing where my time and commitments needed to be, largely because I have this "man thing" about my personality—if I can do something, I don't want another man doing it for me. Even to this day, I don't let the bellman take my luggage when I'm traveling. When he reaches for it, I think, *I don't need you picking up something for me! Put that back down—I've got it!*

Because of this, I tried to carry all of the other responsibilities around the home—mowing the lawn, changing the oil in the car, fixing things—when I was already stretched thin by starting a church, leading my family, going to seminary, and ministering to people. One day I finally had to step back and admit that it was just too much. It was more than I could handle. At that point, I decided to outsource the things that didn't require me personally to do them, such as the lawn care, fixing things around the house, and maintenance on the car. And while that was difficult for me to swallow, it was a choice I had to make in order to free up my time to focus on the things I needed to do—like teach my children God's Word on an ongoing basis. That's no small calling, and it requires time and commitment.[2]

Dr. Evans says that the kingdom parents' first step in passing the baton of faith is making sure their children have an understanding of salvation and make a choice to accept the gifts of forgiveness and eternal life based on Jesus' work on the cross. If you're not sure how to communicate this essential concept to your children, please talk to your class leader or your pastor. Dr. Evans also encourages parents to free up time to teach Bible concepts at home. What is at least one responsibility you can outsource this week so that you can "insource" your children's faith development?

Transformation Moments
Read the following story from 1 Samuel 2. Answer the questions that follow the passage. If you run out of time, finish this section at home.

ELI DROPPED THE BATON

Prologue: A righteous woman named Hannah dedicated her son Samuel to service at the temple when he was very young. Samuel lived at the temple under the care of a priest named Eli. Hannah prayed for her son and visited him once a year.

Now the [two] sons of Eli were worthless men; [Hophni and Phinehas] did not know the LORD . . . The sin of the young men was very great before the LORD, for the men despised the offering of the LORD. . . .

Now Eli was very old; and he heard all that his sons were doing to all Israel, and how they lay with the women who served at the doorway of the tent of meeting. He said to them, "Why do you do such things, the evil things that I hear from all these people? No, my sons; for the report is not good which I hear the LORD's people circulating. If one man sins against another, God will mediate for him; but if a man sins against the LORD, who can intercede for him?" But they would not listen to the voice of their father, for the LORD desired to put them to death.

Now the boy Samuel was growing in stature and in favor both with the LORD and with men.

Then a man of God came to Eli and said to him, "Thus says the LORD, . . . 'Why do you kick at My sacrifice and at My offering which I have commanded in My dwelling, and honor your sons above Me, by making yourselves fat with the choicest of every offering of My people Israel?' Therefore the LORD God of Israel declares, 'I did indeed say that your house and the house of your father should walk before Me forever'; but now the LORD declares, 'Far be it from Me—for those who honor Me I will honor, and those who despise Me will be lightly esteemed. Behold, the days are coming when I will break your strength and the strength of your father's house so that there will not be an old man in your house. . . .This will be the sign to you which will come concerning your two sons, Hophni and Phinehas: on the same day both of them will die. But I will raise up for Myself a faithful priest who will do according to what is in My heart and in My soul; and I will build him an enduring house, and he will walk before My anointed always.'" (1 Samuel 2:12, 17, 22–27, 29–31, 34–36)

How would you describe Eli's failure with his sons, Hophni and Phinehas? What can you deduce about the covenant blessing transfer in Eli's family? Describe the process in which Samuel was blessed.

4

◇ ◇ ◇

Cultivating a Kingdom Atmosphere

The Main Point
Kingdom parents need to create a pleasing atmosphere in the home that attracts their children to kingdom principles.

The Gathering
To find out more about how to create a kingdom atmosphere in your home, read the following excerpt from *Raising Kingdom Kids*. If time allows, discuss the questions that appear at the end of the selection. Or you can finish the section at home.

 ## Hooray for Encouragement
by Dr. Tony Evans

A child needs parents to raise him or her well, not a village. Unless the village has kingdom values, that village will mess up a person. After all, gangs are villages. Entertainment is a village as well. In fact, entertainment is probably the most prevalent village raising kids in our nation today. The average child spends thirty-two or more hours a week in front of the television, tablet, gaming devices, or other forms of electronic media.[1] We don't need more villages raising kids; we need more parents raising kingdom kids.

It is the parents' responsibility to raise their children well, and one of the first ways to do this is by not exasperating them. This means that parents are not to provoke their children. They're not to create irritation, anger, and frustration in the lives of their children. We can easily turn this verse around and say that, rather than discouraging them, parents are to encourage their children.

Scripture tells us, "Death and life are in the power of the tongue" (Proverbs 18:21). A parent who discourages his or her children instead of encouraging them speaks failure and curses into their future. Instead, as parents we are called to give encouragement. There's a difference between encouragement and praise, though. Praise is tied to what a person accomplished. Your child did something you want to acknowledge. Praise is good. But children need encouragement even more. Encouragement is not tied to what they did; it's tied to who they are. Encouragement relates to their identity in Christ and their inheritance as image bearers of God Himself as children of the King.

Have you ever seen a drooping plant quickly perk up when someone pours some water on it? That's what encouragement does. Encouragement will take a droopy kid and perk him or her up again. As the Bible tells us, "Pleasant words are a honeycomb, sweet to the soul and healing to the bones" (Proverbs 16:24). Encouraging your children gives them an expectation of God's goodness and favor on both their todays and their tomorrows. It sets within their hearts an anticipation of a glorious future. Encouragement tells them they are fearfully and wonderfully made and have been gifted by God. It helps them believe that God has a plan for them filled with both a future and a hope.

One reason so many teenagers get caught up with negative groups of their peers today is because that's where their encouragement is found. They get more affirmation from their peers than their parents, and so they respond to that which makes them feel significant. Parents, let your words reach deep into your children's hearts with encouraging truths that communicate to them that you know their personalities, dreams, hopes, struggles and that it will all turn out okay because of who they are and to whom they belong. Give them the hope that they need to face each day.[2]

What was the most encouraging statement your parents ever gave to you? When was the last time you "cheered" for your child when it wasn't a public performance or sporting event? How can creating a home where children hear positive statements foster an atmosphere of spiritual growth?

Show Time!

In session 4 of the *Raising Kingdom Kids Group Video Experience*, Dr. Tony Evans talks about creating a home atmosphere suitable for raising kingdom kids.

◊ ◊ ◊

After viewing Tony Evans's presentation, "Cultivating a Kingdom Atomosphere," use the following questions to help you think through what you saw and heard.

1. Dr. Evans explains that there's a difference between praising our children and encouraging them; praise is acknowledging what a person accomplishes, whereas encouragement is "not tied to what they did; it's tied to who they are." It is connected to "their identity in Christ and their inheritance as image bearers of God Himself as children of the King." In what ways is it easier to praise than encourage?

Write some specific ideas for being more intentional about encouraging your children.

2. Dr. Evans tells us that to "love God, which the Bible says is our first responsibility, is to passionately pursue His glory." It isn't an unrealistic "pie-in-the-sky" idea, but rather to "passionately seek to make Him look good." As a role model for your children, how do you answer Dr. Evans's question, "Are you making God look good?"

In what ways have you fallen short? Check the box of the ones that apply to you or write in your own.
- ❏ spending too much time on work demands
- ❏ focusing more on television or movies
- ❏ spending spare time on computer activities
- ❏ maintaining the household

❒ speaking harshly to others

❒ having a short fuse

❒ being constantly critical or demanding

❒ withholding kind or encouraging comments

❒ withholding affection

❒ other _____

❒ other _____

❒ other _____

3. As we teach our children to love and follow God, we must set up clear boundaries for our children to follow. Yet Dr. Evans strongly reminds us that "rules without relationship will provoke rebellion." In what situations have you dealt with rebellion? How did you respond?

Since we know that hindsight is 20/20, after having listened to Dr. Evans speak to this subject, would you have handled the situations differently? How so?

4. The apostle Paul tells us in Ephesians 6 not to provoke our children to anger, or to exasperate them. Write about a time when your parents exasperated you. Why did it anger you? What can you learn from that experience to apply to your own parenting?

5. Proverbs encourages us to "instruct" our children in the ways of the Lord. Dr. Evans clarifies that by saying it isn't about simply opening a Bible. It means giving our children "God's view of all of life," and doing so in a way that is directed toward each child's particular "bent" or "according to their own unique personality." That means we have to spend time getting to know each of our children and how they are distinct. List each of your children. What are some characteristics that make each unique? In what ways can you "instruct" them in kingdom principles by appealing to their own personalities?

6. Read the following excerpt from *Raising Kingdom Kids,* and reflect on the questions at the end.

STUDY YOUR CHILD
by Dr. Tony Evans

Unfortunately, Proverbs 22:6—"Train up a child in the way he should go, even when he is old he will not depart from it"—is one of the most misinterpreted biblical passages. It is not a promise that if you train up a child in Christian principles, he or she will stay faithful to those principles when he or she is older. This verse means that if you have enough wisdom and insight to train your child according to the unique fingerprints of his or her personality—God-given skills, gifts, and interests—when that child is older, he or she will remain on that path. It is an admonition to parents to study their children well, and then guide them in the direction that best fits their interests and natural abilities.

Had I studied Anthony well, I would have noticed the football lying in the corner of the room under a pile of clothes as an indication of what it truly was: He just wasn't interested in football. I wish I could go back and change what I focused on where he was concerned during those early years, but I can't. And I'm grateful today that he has a thriving music ministry, crossing into both Christian and secular audiences and sharing God's love through the power of his voice. But learn from me—never try to live out your unmet dream through your children. Rather, study your children to recognize their abilities and talents, and then point them in the right direction at a young age. If you do, Scripture tells us that they likely will not depart from it.[3]

Based on this excerpt, what are the benefits of understanding your child's strengths and weaknesses? Jot down your impressions of your child's personality and the way God made him or her.

Transformation Moments
Read the following story from Luke 10. Answer the questions that follow the passage. If you run out of time, finish this section at home.

REWARDING THE RIGHT CHOICES

Now as [Jesus and His disciples] were traveling along, He entered a village; and a woman named Martha welcomed Him into her home. She had a sister called Mary, who was seated at the Lord's feet, listening to His word. But Martha was distracted with all her preparations; and she came up to Him and said, "Lord, do You not care that my sister has left me to do all the serving alone? Then tell her to help me." But the Lord answered and said to her, "Martha, Martha, you are worried and bothered about so many things; but only one thing is necessary, for Mary has chosen the good part, which shall not be taken away from her." (Luke 10:38–42)

How would you describe God's perspective as Jesus looked at Martha's and Mary's choices? In what way did Jesus reward good behavior and model kingdom principles?

5

◇ ◇ ◇

SET A HIGH STANDARD

The Main Point
Parents need to set standards high so that their children become leaders and stand firm in the faith.

The Gathering
To find out more about why we should raise kids with high standards, read the following excerpt from *Raising Kingdom Kids*. If time allows, discuss the questions that appear at the end of the selection. Or you can finish the section at home.

 ## THE KEY TO A HOLY SEX LIFE
by Jonathan Evans

When I was seventeen years old, my father took me out for lunch so we could have a serious, one-on-one conversation about purity. He wanted me to clearly understand God's expectations as I was getting closer to leaving home and going off to college. He explained that God has called me to sanctification—to live and walk as one who believes. He continued explaining that God had not called me to sexual immorality and that impurity was the opposite of being sanctified. He told me that God had a world of living for me to access called godliness, but using the keys of impurity and immorality would not unlock that world. When the conversation was over, he pulled out a little box and slid it across the table for me to open. Inside was a gold necklace with a charm attached to it in the shape of a key. My initial response was certainly that of a typical seventeen–year-old young man. "Dad, this necklace looks like it's for a girl—do you really want me to wear this?"

Fortunately for me, my dad responded by letting me know that it was indeed for a girl. "It's for the girl that God has ordained for you to marry," he explained. He went on to reiterate to me that the key represented access, and had been designed for a specific lock. He explained that this key was to be given only to the woman that I would marry; she would be the God-created lock for my key. He ended our lunch by saying, "Take this key and access the kingdom of godliness rather than breaking into a world of impurity."

Not waiting for the spouse waiting for you in God's kingdom is simply gaining access to a place where you're not welcome. Like a burglar, you may have gotten in, but you won't be there long, and there are always consequences.

Our culture has decided not to use the key of purity, and all these unlawful break-ins have caused chaos in society today. Sexually-transmitted diseases, teenage pregnancies, single parenting, poverty, depression, suicide, and the breakdown of the family—which is the nucleus of the culture—have all been the result. In order to minimize the chaos, we must first minimize the break-ins. It's time for us to teach the next generation the importance of the kingdom key of purity.[1]

What were the standards that Dr. Evans set for his son Jonathan in regard to sexual purity? What were some of the standards in your family of origin in regard to life (not just purity)? Do you have a plan for how to set high standards for your kids? Share your ideas and/or successes with the group.

Show Time!

In session 5 of the *Raising Kingdom Kids Group Video Experience*, Dr. Tony Evans encourages parents to raise a generation of kingdom kids who have kingdom virtue. He challenges parents to raise kids who have integrity.

◊ ◊ ◊

After viewing Tony Evans's presentation "Set a High Standard," use the following questions to help you think through what you saw and heard.

1. Dr. Evans explained the difference between the NFL's rulebook and each team's playbook—how one offers the boundaries within which every player must operate and how the other takes those boundaries into consideration and applies the principles to different situations within the actual game. So it is with God's rulebook, the Bible, and your family's playbook. As you teach your children the boundaries of the rulebook, you must also instruct them in the wisdom of how to apply each principle to specific situations. In what ways do you instill the kingdom virtue of wisdom in your children so they can make strong, good decisions?

2. Dr. Evans tells about a time when he bit into a wax apple, thinking it was real because it looked so juicy and appealing. Too often our children can clean up nicely on the outside, but

not have a pure heart. We want to instill integrity and purity into their character. In what ways have you tried to teach your children about the importance and power of integrity and honesty?

Do you encourage them when you see your children act out those traits? If not, would you make that part of your parenting playbook? Why or why not?

3. Dr. Evans said, "Faith is measured by your feet not by your feelings." In your own words, write how you would explain that concept to your children.

4. Dr. Evans claims that faith grows through obstacles. What are some obstacles people in the Bible had to face? What are some of the life obstacles you have dealt with? Did you rise to the challenge or not? What lesson can you teach your children about either outcome?

5. Kerri Strug and other athletes offer examples of *physical* resiliency. Who are people in your life who have modeled *faith* resiliency? When can you set aside some time to tell your kids about those faithful people who have influenced you?

6. Read the following excerpt from *Raising Kingdom Kids*, and reflect on the questions at the end.

YOU GOT TO SERVE SOMEBODY

by Dr. Tony Evans

It's hard to find full-service gas stations anymore unless you are in the Pacific Northwest; most stations throughout the US offer self-service only. I remember the days when someone would come out to pump the gas, wash the windows, and check the oil and the tires. Not anymore—in fact, these days you rarely see anyone at all. You just swipe your credit card, fill up your tank, and head on your way.

Unfortunately, what is true for filling stations nowadays is also true for God's people in many ways. Instead of individuals coming to worship service, they now show up to "worship selfish" . . . because it's all about them. They want the benefits and blessings of the kingdom without investing and serving in the kingdom. While there is nothing wrong with benefits or blessings in and of themselves, I find nothing in the Bible that says a blessing is ever to stop with the one being blessed. A blessing is always meant to go through—not just to—someone in order to benefit others as well. Our kids are growing up in a "me generation" like never before. Social media and easy access to so many things have cultivated in them a spirit that seeks to be instantly gratified as if that were normal. . . .

Far too many of our children have been raised with a distorted prince and princess mentality that causes them to believe that the world in which they walk rotates around them. Upon reaching adulthood, though, they will receive a rude awakening. Not only does the real world not operate that way, neither does God's kingdom. We are royalty in God's kingdom, but His kingdom is not the Magic Kingdom—in God's kingdom Christ has called us to roll up our shirtsleeves and serve.

The Jesus who came to give us life abundantly is the same Jesus who asks us to take up our cross, and do so daily. Service ought to be a way of life—a service mind-set in both you and your children because we were created to serve. We read in Ephesians, "For we are His workmanship, created in Christ Jesus for good works, which God prepared beforehand so that we would walk in them" (2:10). Good works involve actions or activities that benefit others while bringing glory to God. Essentially, good works mean service. . . .

In Galatians we read, "For you were called to freedom, brethren; only do not turn your freedom into an opportunity for the flesh, but through love serve one another" (5:13). One way we express our identity in Christ is through service. The freedom Jesus purchased for us on the cross is meant to be the catalyst for our service. A non-serving Christian is a contradiction.[2]

Based on this excerpt, we know that a kingdom mind-set involves service. In what ways do you serve your children? your spouse? Your fellow church members? What are some practical ways your family unit can serve the community? What are some ways your children can individually serve others?

Transformation Moments

Read the following story from Acts 9. Answer the questions that follow the passage. If you run out of time, finish this section at home.

 ## AN EARLY CHURCH SERVANT

Now in Joppa there was a disciple named Tabitha (which translated in Greek is called Dorcas); this woman was abounding with deeds of kindness and charity which she continually did. And it happened at that time that she fell sick and died; and when they had washed her body, they laid it in an upper room. Since Lydda was near Joppa, the disciples, having heard that Peter was there, sent two men to him, imploring him, "Do not delay in coming to us." So Peter arose and went with them. When he arrived, they brought him into the upper room; and all the widows stood beside him, weeping and showing all the tunics and garments that Dorcas used to make while she was with them. But Peter sent them all out and knelt down and prayed, and turning to the body, he said, "Tabitha, arise." And she opened her eyes, and when she saw Peter, she sat up. And he gave her his hand and raised her up; and calling the saints and widows, he presented her alive. It became known all over Joppa, and many believed in the Lord. And Peter stayed many days in Joppa with a tanner named Simon. (Acts 9:36–43)

What are the gifts that are usually recognized in the church? Why are gifts of service often overlooked? Do you know the name of your church's groundskeeper? Which would you consider the greater act—Peter healing Tabitha or Tabitha's lifelong service to the community? (Explain your answer.)

6

◇ ◇ ◇

Raising Royal Kids

The Main Point

No matter what happened in the past, kingdom parents can effectively raise royal kids who are fit for a kingdom legacy.

The Gathering

To find out more about why we should raise kids with the standards of royalty, read the following excerpt from *Raising Kingdom Kids*. If time allows, discuss the questions that appear at the end of the selection. Or you can finish the section at home.

 ## Abandon Mediocrity
by Dr. Tony Evans

Kingdom parents, if you are satisfied with your kids being mediocre, then mediocre might be all that you are going to get. If you don't raise the bar, how can your kids experience anything better? You run the risk of them becoming mediocre adults who marry mediocre spouses because that's all your kids know and understand. But if you raise the bar, what might happen? Your kids could become the cream of the crop—aiming for excellence in all things.

These days, in a room that is crowded with no more seats available, it amazes me that men will allow women to stand for an inordinate amount of time. My father would have corrected me sternly if I ever let a woman stand for an extended period of time while I was seated. Today we've got a generation of children being raised without the simplest notions of etiquette, common courtesy, respect, honor, excellence, and integrity. Why? Because we have a generation of parents who are so distracted by the sights, sounds, and smells of life's adventures that they simply settle for mediocrity in both themselves and their offspring. It's easier that way. However, trifling children typically grow up to become trifling adults—and, in the long run, that isn't easy at all.

Obviously not everyone is going to excel in everything. Raising kingdom kids who are "choice" simply means they will maximize their personal potential and God-given gifts. Maybe they won't be in the top of their particular class in every subject, but whatever it is that God has created them to fulfill, they will do so with a degree of excellence, and they will do all else to the best of their abilities.[1]

What does it mean to you to raise kids to perform "to the best of their abilities"? What are some of the discourtesies you see in our culture? Why should you raise your children to have excellent standards in a culture where behavior like "trolling" (being rude on the Internet) is an acceptable and applauded pastime?

Show Time!

In session 6 of the *Raising Kingdom Kids Group Video Experience*, Dr. Tony Evans opens his talk by describing the process of building a foundation for a skyscraper. He compares the hard work of building a strong foundation for a building to raising a strong kingdom kid. He encourages parents to put a lot of effort into raising kids.

◊ ◊ ◊

After viewing Tony Evans's presentation, "Raising Royal Kids," use the following questions to help you think through what you saw and heard.

1. Sometimes we can become so busy trying to survive that we forget the importance of expecting our children to be the best they can be. We settle for "good enough." But Dr. Evans says as kingdom people, we have no room for mediocrity. What are some things in your life that keep you from setting the bar high for your children? Check the box of the ones that apply to you or write your own.

   ❐ Too tired. Work keeps me busy.

   ❐ Too scheduled. We have too many things going on.

   ❐ No good role model. My parents didn't push me, so I'm not sure how to set appropriate expectations for my kids.

   ❐ Guilt. I want my kids to like me, not feel pressured to "perform."

   ❐ I don't see the importance. I love my kids just as they are.

   ❐ other _____

   ❐ other _____

   ❐ other _____

2. Dr. Evans said, "Today we've got a generation of children being raised without the simplest notions of etiquette, common courtesy, respect, honor, excellence, and integrity." They simply

don't know that they are royalty and need to behave as such. In what ways have you perhaps been lax in teaching your children about common respectful behavior and integrity? What simple steps can you take today to begin to teach your children and expect them to act with honor and courtesy?

3. Dr. Evans told the story about how the young elephants in South Africa had lost their parents to poachers and they were running wild, until researchers introduced bull elephants into their midst and calmed down all the young elephants. Does this story apply to your family? If so, in what ways?

Are there single parents in your church or community who could use some "bull elephants" to help train and bring excellence and high expectations about behavior back to the home?

4. If you were to die today, what spiritual legacy would you leave behind? Is that the legacy you most want to leave?

Dr. Evans encourages us to write our spiritual wills now because we need to know what we're going to set in motion "for when [we're] no longer here to carry them to the next level." Have you written your spiritual legacy? What's stopping you from leaving a written testament to what you want your children and grandchildren to become? Start writing the first draft of that will.

5. Dr. Evans told about the biblical story of Asher, one of Jacob's twelve sons, and how he redeemed his past to leave a great spiritual legacy for his children. In what ways is your past holding you captive, keeping you back from leaving a strong legacy? What lesson can you apply from Asher's life to redeem your past and move forward in power and strength to influence your children to be great leaders?

6. Read the following excerpt from *Raising Kingdom Kids*, and reflect on the questions at the end.

THEY CALL ME "MOMMY"
by Chrystal Evans Hurst

They call me Mommy. It's a five-letter word that my children use all day, every day, hundreds and thousands of times a day. And it means . . .

I need you . . .

I'm hurting . . .

Help me . . .

Can we talk? . . .

Love me . . . and

What's for dinner?

They use that word so loosely. They use that word a lot. They use it whenever they need to find me.

Why? Because they know that I hold the keys.

They know I hold the keys to whatever will make it onto their dinner plates that evening.

They know that if anybody can get the splinter out, I can.

They know that if anyone will love them, I will.

But that common name means so much more. It means that I am responsible, along with my husband, for training them in righteousness. It means that I have to shape their hearts and their character in a way that will prepare them for the plans God has for their lives. It means that they will learn from me how they are to parent their own children someday.

And it's scary.

It's a little unsettling to think that you could mess up your kids, isn't it?

I know I'm not perfect, but somehow that fact is grossly magnified under the lens of my role in the lives of my family.

Asher's story comforts me. He didn't get it right at first either.

And then, when he grew up and became a man, he didn't have the picture-perfect family. But that didn't stop his children from becoming leaders characterized by bravery, excellence, and influence.

My parents did a great job raising us. Really. They did. They will tell you that they don't harbor many regrets. That's wonderful to hear.

But I want to encourage those who may be reading this book on raising kingdom kids and thinking, *Well, this couldn't apply to me. I've messed up too badly to be a positive influence in the lives of my children.*

Enter Asher.

He messed up too. After bad decisions, he committed himself to make good ones going forward.

Enter the blended family.

A perfectly nuclear family was not a prerequisite for God to work through Asher to produce godly people.

Enter impact.

As I've heard my father say many times, "God can hit a bull's-eye with a crooked stick." And while Asher—and maybe you and I—may not have had a straight start, God can work miracles.

So as you read this book and arm yourself with knowledge to help you in your parenting journey . . .

Know that when your children call out for you, Mommy and Daddy are not titles to be held loosely.

You are not common.

You hold a crucial place and have significant value in the life of your children, now and in the future they will experience.

And if you choose, starting now, to have a kingdom home, you can have an impact beyond your wildest dreams.[2]

Based on this excerpt, no parent is perfect. How does the concept of God hitting a bull's-eye "with a crooked stick" encourage you? What would you say to someone who wanted to become a more influential parent?

Transformation Moments

Read the following passage from the book of 1 Peter. Answer the questions that follow the passage. If you run out of time, finish this section at home.

A ROYAL PRIESTHOOD

Putting aside all malice and all deceit and hypocrisy and envy and all slander, like newborn babies, long for the pure milk of the word, so that by it you may grow in respect to salvation, if you have tasted the kindness of the Lord.

And coming to Him as to a living stone which has been rejected by men, but is choice and precious in the sight of God, you also, as living stones, are being built up as a spiritual house for a holy priesthood, to offer up spiritual sacrifices acceptable to God through Jesus Christ. For this is contained in Scripture:

"Behold, I lay in Zion a choice stone, a precious corner stone, and he who believes in Him will not be disappointed."

This precious value, then, is for you who believe; but for those who disbelieve, "The stone which the builders rejected, this became the very corner stone," and, "A stone of stumbling and a rock of offense"; for they stumble because they are disobedient to the word, and to this doom they were also appointed.

But you are a chosen race, a royal priesthood, a holy nation, a people for God's own possession, so that you may proclaim the excellencies of Him who has called you out of darkness into His marvelous light; for you once

were not a people, but now you are the people of God; you had not received
mercy, but now you have received mercy. (1 Peter 2:1–10)

This passage from 1 Peter reminds us of who we are in Christ. What
are some standards parents can teach their children to practice as
being members of "a chosen race, a royal priesthood, a holy nation,
a people for God's own possession"? How does the last paragraph
apply to raising kingdom kids?

NOTES

Session 1: This Isn't the Magic Kingdom

1. Adapted from Tony Evans, *Raising Kingdom Kids* (Carol Stream, IL: Tyndale, 2014), 5.
2. Priscilla Shirer quoted in Tony Evans, *Raising Kingdom Kids*, 6–7.

Session 2: "But Daniel . . ."

1. Tony Evans, *Raising Kingdom Kids* (Carol Stream, IL: Tyndale, 2014), 57.
2. Anthony Evans Jr. quoted in Tony Evans, *Raising Kingdom Kids*, 50–1.

Session 3: Transfer the Kingdom Baton

1. Tony Evans, *Raising Kingdom Kids* (Carol Stream, IL: Tyndale, 2014), 226–7.
2. Tony Evans, *Raising Kingdom Kids*, 33–4.

Session 4: Cultivating a Kingdom Atmosphere

1. Kyla Boyse, "Television and Children," University of Michigan Health System, last updated August 2010, http://www.med.umich.edu/yourchild/topics/tv.htm.

2. Adapted from Tony Evans, *Raising Kingdom Kids* (Carol Stream, IL: Tyndale, 2014), 95–96.

3. Adapted from Tony Evans, *Raising Kingdom Kids* (Carol Stream, IL: Tyndale, 2014), 87–8.

Session 5: Set a High Standard

1. Jonathan Evans quoted in Tony Evans, *Raising Kingdom Kids* (Carol Stream, IL: Tyndale, 2014), 203.

2. Adapted from Tony Evans, *Raising Kingdom Kids*, 207–8.

Session 6: Raising Royal Kids

1. Adapted from Tony Evans, *Raising Kingdom Kids* (Carol Stream, IL: Tyndale, 2014), 25–6.

2. Chrystal Evans Hurst quoted in Tony Evans, *Raising Kingdom Kids*, 22–3.

About the Author

DR. TONY EVANS is the founder and president of The Urban Alternative, a national ministry dedicated to restoring hope in personal lives, families, churches, and communities. Dr. Evans also serves as senior pastor of Oak Cliff Bible Fellowship in Dallas. He is a best-selling author of numerous books, and his radio program, *The Alternative with Dr. Tony Evans*, is heard daily on more than 500 radio stations. Dr. Evans is also the chaplain for the Dallas Mavericks and former chaplain for the Dallas Cowboys. For more information, visit *TonyEvans.org*.